High Income, Z Strategies for Network Marketers

Easy, Effective, and Free Ways on How to Boost Your Network Marketing Business

By: Leanne Toinette Higgins

9781681279466

PUBLISHERS NOTES

Disclaimer – Speedy Publishing LLC

This book was originally printed before 2014. This is an adapted reprint by Speedy Publishing LLC with newly updated content designed to help readers with much more accurate and timely information and data.

Speedy Publishing LLC

40 E Main Street, Newark, Delaware, 19711

Contact Us: 1-888-248-4521

Website: http://www.speedypublishing.co

REPRINTED Paperback Edition: 9781681279466:

Manufactured in the United States of America

DEDICATION

This book is dedicated to my partner in crime and in life, my husband, Jeremy.

TABLE OF CONTENTS

CHAPTER 1- MAKE PROFITS WITHIN WEEKS OF BUSINESS CREATION

What is the purpose of starting a business? To make profit. Most businesses spend more money than they make that's why they go belly up. So why should network marketing be any different? The common belief is that network marketing is a business that appreciates in value over time. In other words, if I have a group of 100 to 1,000 people under me buying the product and recruiting more, I'd be getting richer and richer! But we all know that.

It is not the pot of gold at the end of the rainbow. It's surviving the first 6 months to 2 years! It is common that most network marketers in a new industry typically go through a 6 months trial and error period, therefore, it is crucial to ensure that during those 6 training months, you manage your cash wisely so you can learn and make money at the same time.

Just like in normal business, most of them fail within their first 2 years of operation and struggle to make profit even if they do survive. The key to survival is cash flow. In other words, it can be summed up in this equation: cash today, downlines tomorrow.

People in network marketing usually run out of cash flow normally after 3 months and they quit because they spend more as they build. But by breaking even as fast as possible, it gives tremendous mental strength to the distributor and he or she is less likely to drop out. First, we must understand the mindset which is the most important starting point in getting by the first 3 months.

How Does a Business Builder Think?

- It takes time to build a successful business. If you make any money in the first few months (even if it is just a few dollars) it is perfectly normal.

- It is my business. Not my upline's business or my downline's business. Everything depends on me putting effort to succeed.

- Invest in tools that bring in revenue (lead generators, viral e-books, generic information, etc.). Don't buy books and tapes just for the sake of buying them. • don't use your own money if possible. Most successful businessmen use other people's money (borrowed money either from relatives or financial institutions) to build their business. Remember that cash flow is more important than revenue.

- Don't blow all your money on advertising that doesn't bring in cash flow as well. Direct response advertising is one of the most effective ways.

- A smart businessman doesn't spread himself out too much. Build the local market first. Never venture outstation unless you have a steady income. If you can't even take care of yourself, how can you take care of your downlines far away from you?

- Focus on solving other people's problems. Don't recruit people just for the sake of recruiting them. Try and understand what problems they are going through first.

- Enjoying the journey! People who love their job always outperform those who do it grudgingly. If your prospect sees you doing your business so grudgingly, will they join you?

The Usual MLM Cash Flow

Typical average American worker's annual salary:

In an hour $19.13

In a day $153.04

In a month $3,316.25

In a year $39,795

Minus expenses expected of a network marketer:

Joining fee $50 - $5,000

Auto-ship $5 - $500

Petrol $300

Training materials $200 - $500

Meetings and rallies $50 - $8,000

Phone bill $100 - $500

Leads $200 - $500

Miscellaneous $200 - $500

Depending on the network marketing company, do you see how typical it is for an average builder to spend somewhere between $1,000 and $16,000 as a starting investment? You can estimate how much you have to make in the long run then only will you break even. But let us see how we can minimize these overheads to generate more cash flow.

CHAPTER 2- YOUR REAL PROFIT MARGIN

The Compensation Plan

Different plans may differ from company to company. Some companies may boast of their high payout. They will say something like this:

Our company is the best because we pay out 75% of our commission to all the distributors! It is like saying for every $100 sale; $75 is paid back to our people. You will never fail with this company!

I urge you to make intelligent financial decisions and NOT emotional decisions because responding to emotional appeal can cause a lot of heartaches in the future.

But for the purpose of this topic, I will list down some principles (marketing plan related) to follow.

- Don't look at the total payout of the company; look at the first 2 levels of payout:

  How much you get for recruiting someone, and how much you get if THEY recruit someone. It is no point dreaming how much you make as a 'Rainbow Diamond Leader' if you can't even succeed at the lower levels

- Examine how much you have to spend to RECRUIT someone. Some companies require you to either pay for their training program first, or require you to accompany them into the training session (and you have to pay your own way)

- If you have little cash flow but wish to join a company that requires a large inventory investment but high profit margin, make sure those products can be used to SPONSOR your downlines so you can recuperate as much cash as possible

- Can you afford the auto-ship?

Do You Need Downlines to Grow Your Business?

What is the income you are expecting from your business? Do you know that you have to invest time and money in your downlines? Yes, it is true that you make money when your downlines joins you or makes a sale, but most of the time, to build a long term business; you have to invest heavily in their education.

Network Marketing is a business of duplication and although many people will pay the price to build their network, you must be very selective of whom you spend your time with. You can't possibly be everything to everyone and you must select who are the people that you are going places with! It makes sense because they time you spend with one means time where you could either be developing another or recruiting a new distributor.

Furthermore, you have to drive out of your house to see them or accompany them in training and counseling sessions. Are you prepared to pay the price for 'this guy'? Most of the time many people quit network marketing is not because they can't recruit, but because they spend too much time with a recruit thinking they can change a duck into an eagle.

You quack with ducks but soar with eagles, if I am not mistaken. So if you spend too much time with a duck that quacks a lot but doesn't do anything else, you have no choice but to leave him behind if you need to soar with the eagles (or else you will be like the 'duck' as well).

The key point to remember is this: If you are doing 99% of the work in your network while the rest is doing 1%: START FINDING NEW DOWNLINES, They will spend less of your money (and free up your time to make more).

How to Eliminate the Big Expenses

Here is a step by step instruction to ways you can tackle the expenditure above. Joining fee and auto-ship: Instead of going out to start looking for people to join your opportunity, one of the fastest ways to ensure cash flow is to LIQUIDATE your products! See that stash of products lying around your house? (Your health supplements, skin care or water filters, etc.)

A lot of people leave their stocks lying around the house while going on a recruitment spree forgetting that once you sell off all your stocks, you will break even on your investment! If you are wondering whether to keep those products so you can try them yourself, don't worry. There is more where that came from. If you work hard to eliminate your investment costs, you can always purchase more products from the company later on and those products will most likely contribute to your sales volume as well.

The key is to get your WARM MARKET started on the products, and not pitch the opportunity to them straight away! If you try a good product at the supermarket, I am sure you will tell them all about it. Why should you treat your network marketing products any different? Are you afraid to talk to your uncle bob because your products are from a network marketing company?

Once you get your family and friends started on the products (It doesn't cost you that much considering that those are money set aside for your business whether you sell or give them away), once they see results from it, they will start promoting the products to the people around them!

Don't you see how by using your inventory when you first started off, you can potentially create runaway word of mouth giving you free warm leads offline? The best thing of all, you can choose from those groups of product users who can be a good business builder because of their trust in the product, you can get them in easily.

Doing so will also eliminate your costs when it comes to auto-ship. When people are actively consuming the product, all your downlines will be on auto-ship and you will not be afraid of them canceling their auto-ship because it is taken care off by their warm market demand.

If you want to be successful in network marketing, your must invest in yourself. No I don't mean investing in stuff that goes below your neck because there is a tendency for network marketers to eat a lot during group gatherings (and grow sideways!): It is investing in what's above your neck which is your mind! Serious network marketers will always invest their hard-earned money in two things.

• Leads

• Training Materials to upgrade themselves like books and tapes

Since we know that people will be spending money on the second category, why not make a profit from it to fund your business? One of the ways is to obtain training materials is to join free membership sites that provide free e-books or training material to help you expand your knowledge. These low cost, methods will help you tremendously instead of spending your much needed funds for surviving in your business on expensive hard-cover books that will cost $50-$300.

One website I highly recommend to generate leads online for free is Mike Dillard's Magnetic Sponsoring 10 day's boot camp. This boot camp offers a training system especially tailored for network marketers.

The best thing about it is that it is FREE and 100% generic and works with any company. His website comes with a built in lead capture system which will allow you to build relationships with your prospects as well as generate additional cash flow for your downlines. You can promote this system down your genealogy chart so that everybody will benefit from the cash flow.

Phone Bills

As soon as your network begins to grow, you must consider switching to a phone plan that provides low-cost or unlimited access to all sub-lines. This is a great way to save on phone bills when calling your downlines.

Some telephone companies offer unique phone plans that give you a referral fee or even an overriding percentage over your referee's or your network's bill. Other ways to cut down on phone bills is to go online to coordinate team meetings over the internet. Tools like Skype are useful to do long distance opportunity meetings and counseling sessions with your upline.

Petrol

If you find yourself burning too much petrol when prospecting, then you must consider

QUALIFYING your leads.

Not everyone who gets into your group will be a 'CLASS A' networker. It is wise to focus on recruiting people who have qualities to succeed in any business. Opportunities do not make someone rich; hard work and persistence does.

If you are prospecting someone who is indecisive, lazy and complains constantly, it is better to keep him or her in the back burner and focus on other people (follow up with them on your spare time). You don't want to find yourself driving miles just to talk to someone and after two hours (or a few months later) you find out that they are not interested or they are not the person you are looking for.

Leanne Toinette Higgins

A very good way to qualify what type of prospect you are dealing with if to ask him or her questions about their self-development. If you find that they have no energy in their words, or are not doing anything to improve them then you can very well save lots of time and petrol.

Leads

You don't have to spend a fortune on leads. Here are some suggestions on how to get leads for free.

• Switching to a line of work that allows you flexible time and involves servicing instead of moving to a sales oriented line. Why is this so is because a servicing oriented line allows you to build rapport for free with your prospects and they will generally have good feelings towards you contrary to a sales line where the same customers you are selling your product will wind up being the same prospects for your business (Don't confuse them by selling many things).

• Other network marketing companies. Join their Opportunity talks or rallies. You will get to know many like-minded people here and there and they will be more than happy to be your friend because they want to get you into their opportunity. You can sort and filter which are the people you want in your network later on. If your convincing power is very good, you might bring over an entire network of distributors over.

• Attend highly motivational seminars (e.g. Anthony Robbins), you will meet a lot of people here and they will be so highly motivated or fired-up, you will have more chances to recruit them (they are so fired-up they believe they can conquer the world or realize their dreams). Furthermore, they are most likely the ones who will 'go all the way' if you successfully recruit them.

CHAPTER 3- DEVELOP MULTIPLE STREAMS OF INCOME

A lot of network marketers make a very big mistake in their business. They don't develop multiple streams of incomes and they rely only on making money through one source which is the company they are in. What do I mean?

Let's say I am with Xyz Company. I feel that Xyz Company has the best reputation in the world, the best product, the best marketing plan, has helped millions of people in the world with the product and opportunity (you get the idea). Because I am so engrossed with my company, I refuse to engage other streams of income like buying or endorsing the other products of other companies. Some even go as far as to learn only within their own network marketing community only. Let me emphasize once again.

The Business of Network Marketing

You must be receptive to new ideas and constantly learn (even from other network marketing companies!) As a businessman, you must be savvy enough to adapt to situations and do whatever it takes (as long as it is ethical) to get the job done. This means that your thinking must be flexible enough to come out with ideas that accomplish the following steps:

• generate endless leads so you will have a large name list

• create consistent cash flow to stay alive in network marketing

• recruit downlines and train them to execute all these steps

How do we accomplish the following steps?

(1) Adopt the mindset of abundance. Help other people to get what they want and next time, they will definitely help you get what you want. Go all out to help others and don't be stingy or calculative.

(2) Focus on developing a customer base by servicing them through the product. Focus on solving their problems with the product. Even if you have to spend time to build the rapport with the customer, remember that when the customer sees fantastic results from your product, they will sell for you willingly.

A satisfied customer's testimonial is very powerful. Repeat sales from the satisfied customer (and the people around them) will ensure a consistent cash flow.

(3) Barter-trade your company's product with networkers from other companies! If I have loads of stock from my company (either through purchasing in bulk or from my auto-ship), chances are, there are networkers in other companies are more than willing to trade with you since they have loads of stock also.

With new types of stock in your hand, you are able to tap into other markets and build rapport with them so you can introduce them to your main opportunity. (If my company only sells cosmetics and no supplements, I can find a networker in the supplement like and exchange products to tap the supplement market.)

(4) Join affiliate programs online that generate cash flow if you are internet savvy. Find affiliate programs that let you participate for a very low cost or free. Remember the principle that you want to generate cash flow and help other people solve their problems. This puts you in a position to once again, build rapport with your potential prospects and generates you leads. Viral marketing using e-books or e-mail is a good way to divert traffic to your affiliate programs and they cost very little.

(5) Give away free information on network marketing (there are lots of free or low cost e-books or viral marketing tools around the net) or write free articles on your products and post them to your friends, associates or families.

For example: if you are in the health industry, write (or interview an expert) an article about general health issues or health supplements that will give your potential prospects awareness on their health and when they are curious they will ask you for more information. You can share your product with them afterwards.

Network Marketing is a business for you but not by you.

Although there no hard and fast rule or any magic formula that I can suggest, because any system you decide to create will differ from company to company, you can develop your own turn-key system within your organization. What this means is this kind of system is designed with the team in mind where you and all your downlines all follow the same system as a general outline.

Everybody needs to head in the same direction as a team and a single minded focus on achieving the team objective is crucial. Here are some guidelines I can suggest to you:

• Hold local training sessions besides the company's training sessions online or offline with all your team members

• Educate all the team members about proper cash flow guidelines when building the business. Give everyone free material to review.

• Everyone decide how much effort must be put in, for example, a weekly or monthly target volume to achieve.

• Training sessions on how to use online systems that generate leads or using affiliate websites (if your company sponsors one). You may even work together to create your own team website.

• Buddy system to minimize prospecting costs (like driving to the meetings together or prospecting together)

• Brainstorming ideas on other ways to save costs (for example: joining a phone plan together as mentioned above)

High Income, Zero Debt Strategies for Network Marketers

The key point to remember is this: Everyone must focus on following the same system in your team! It is crucial for duplication. Can you imagine 100 people all going in their own direction? It smells like a recipe for disaster.

The ultimate goal is to train a team of independent, cash generating downlines who are making money and helping their downlines to do the same.

At the end of the day, how good your turn-key system turns out reflects heavily on you through the success of your downlines.

What is the point of sponsoring 10-20 people, and the next week there is only 1 or 2 left in the business? If attrition is very high in your network, it is even more so to create a system for your downlines.

CHAPTER 4- CONSIDER VIRAL MARKETING

Ever had Chicken Pox? It all starts from one member of the family getting infected by a friend or a relative. He brings the virus home and pretty soon the entire family gets hit by chicken pox... but not before the 'carrier' passes it to another friend's family!

This is what viral marketing is like – when you have the necessary tools to drive traffic to your website, your profits will be unstoppable! It becomes even more powerful when applied in network marketing.

- Here are a few key components you will need to accomplish this feat: Advertisements placed in strategic locations (e.g. at the back of viral E-books)

- E-products with resell rights (any form that allows the product to be easily passed to another – master resell rights, unrestricted PLR rights, rebranding rights or giveaway rights)

- Viral software to refer your friends (e.g. Viral Friend Generator)

Get the Right "Carrier"

If you want to kick start your viral marketing campaign you will need to find a suitable 'carrier' for your 'viruses'.

By having the right carrier, you will be able to launch your campaign as swiftly as possible because it will take a while before the viral effect starts to kick in.

A suitable carrier would be an E-product that will easily fall into the hands of many readers automatically and it must have a targeted audience (related to that particular niche) who will find your ad useful.

However, you must choose the right kind of carrier. This carrier must either have a lot of credibility or an attraction factor that will appeal to the target audience or the resellers (other carriers).

An example of an effective carrier is that the E-product must have an appealing E-cover that will capture the attention of your prospects.

You must give them a reason to do the viral marketing work for you without you doing it yourself. The key is to set it up correctly the first time (choosing the best product to place your ad, writing a compelling advertisement and choosing the best placements).

Then, when your campaign launches, you won't need to do anything more other than watch the traffic flow in!

Get Your "Sales Force" to Sell for You – For Free!

Now that you have found your 'carrier', 95% of the work will be done by your 'sales force' while you sit back and watch them spread the love.

They will promote the carriers for their own profit or benefit, while your ads and your links are sitting cozily in their books.

Here are a few examples of how the viral effect works out in the form of your E-products:

- Unrestricted PLR E-books or special reports. The easier it is for people to get their hands on your book, the better the traffic! Do not worry about people altering your ads – people are usually too lazy to alter the book. They will promote your links for you! The most appealing thing about unrestricted PLR is that people can SELL the PLR rights to others making it highly valuable!

- E-books or special reports with Master resell rights. The same applies as unrestricted PLR. Resellers can resell your books, bundle your books together as a package or into a fire sale or offer them as a bonus. You can watch as your books (and your links) fall into the hands of readers all over the world!

- Products with giveaway rights. If you have excellent content, people are more than willing to give away your book to others and the virus spreads. Although it carries less perceived value compared to a 'paid' product, nevertheless, it still has its usefulness if your content is good.

You can create as many viral campaigns as you can for your website. Once they are all setup, all you need to do is tweak your sales pages or landing pages to maximize your profits.

CHAPTER 5- WHAT ARE FIRE SALES?

A Great Source for Paid Leads

What better way to get highly targeted traffic other than being a contributor for a fire sale!

If you don't know what a fire sale is, it is a special type of sale with three important characteristics:

• Time limited (only last for a couple of days)

• Rock bottom pricing (but full of value)

• And it all comes with a theme

So what does that got to do with getting paid leads?

The nature of Fire Sales requires the merchant to sell tons of valuable products for a rock bottom price. Therefore, they would want to provide as much value for the prospects as possible in order to guarantee a sale.

In order to maximize the value, the merchant either:

- Sources for products on his own

- Or he can do it the easy way by asking contributors to add their own products to the fire sale!

If you know about a fire sale going on, what you can do is to ask the merchant if you can add your own product as a bonus. Normally, they will allow the buyers to download your product by directing them to your landing page!

This is pulled off within a limited time frame so the scarcity factor involved. Paid leads are also very valuable because they are highly targeted traffic. The fact that they are willing to pay money to buy Internet marketing products shows that they are serious about making money online.

No Hard Selling Required!

One of the best things about being a contributor for fire sales is the fact that you do not need to exert additional effort in collecting paid leads.

Firstly, because people are already pre-sold on the idea that your product is of value and they will gladly opt-in to download your product.

You don't need to do a lot of 'convincing' either on your landing page or lead-capture form. All you need to do is write a simple,

"Download here, exclusively for the subscribers of the Fire Sale!" and it will suffice!

Furthermore, there is always a theme involved with every Fire Sale. A good theme ensures that the subscribers are all willing to help you out and buy your product (if they are not sold on the idea of the product's value, at the very least, they will support your reason for holding the fire sale and buy from you).

For example:

There was one highly successful Fire Sale executed during the year of 2007 called Send Us to U.S.

The theme was to send 3 desperate guys from Malaysia to the U.S. by funding their trip through the fire sale.

This garnered a lot of support all around the Internet community and people everywhere are contributing products and buying their package – the traffic they got is huge and if you happened to be a contributor to their fire sale, imagine the number of people downloading your product by opting in at your landing page!

CHAPTER 6 - WRITE OR FIND SOMEONE WHO CAN

- **High Traffic Blogs**

Blogging is one of the BEST tools for network marketing distributors!

How does one maximize from a high traffic blog when that blog doesn't belong to you or when your own blog has little traffic to begin with? How does one cope when he is new to Internet marketing?

Well, one of the fastest ways to get started out is to search for blogs that are constantly looking for content from contributors like the blog on the previous page.

The Marketing Blog Zine talks about Internet marketing and making money online. It provides targeted traffic for anyone who wants to learn about Internet marketing.

If you want to divert traffic from blogs like these, what you can do is to contribute your own blog posts as a contributor.

Talk about topics that are relevant to their blog as well as your own. This is a good way to capture the reader's attention.

You will reap the following benefits:

• You get to tap into their traffic and drive traffic to your website

• You get to build your credibility online because you get to leverage on their 'authority'

• The blog post remains there for a certain period of time ensuring that you will get maximum exposure

Contribute Relevant Content

As mentioned above regarding credibility, there is one section that you must take note of because it is really valuable.

Beneath every article that you contribute, there is a section called the author's bio. This bio books allows you to 'sell' yourself and brand yourself as an expert in whatever niche that you are in.

A sample bio looks something like this:

===
Article ©2007 Khai, all rights reserved. Khai is a product creation expert, copywriter and E-consultant. He has created HUNDREDS of

E-products online within a span of 10 short months and has a strong passion for writing. For a dose of his writings & newsletter, check out his blog at (website).

==

Use this bio box wisely and you can be sure to drive tons of traffic to your website!

• Relevant Article Directories

Have you read the newspaper only to get the feeling that the very article that you are reading is already published all over the Internet for a long time?

Those articles are probably taken from article directories from the Internet, and yet it is a viable source for information on any niche!

If you want to drive tons of traffic to your website using a free or low cost way, then article directory submissions are the to go!

Why article marketing is so lucrative is because of the following reasons:

• Famous article directories have LOTS of targeted traffic. Thousands of people go to article directories to source for content (e.g. for your local newspaper).

• Similar to high traffic blogs, article directories also allow you to brand yourself as an expert.

• Some article directories rank high on the search engines – it allows your author bio to rank high on the SERP (search engine result page) and it even passes the PR (page rank) juice to your websites.

Write an article about product or something related to your website. (If you can't write, don't worry… you can pay someone as low as $5 to get a quality article written for you).

Once your article is complete, do a search on Google for the search term – "article directory".

You will find a list of article directories.

Choose one of them and register as an author or an article writer and contribute your article to the directory. It might take a few days or even a week to get an article approved, so make sure you are patient enough to wait.

Once your article is approved, it will remain on the 'front page' of that particular niche for a couple of days before it is 'pushed down' by newer article submissions.

Rinse and Repeat

One of the advantages of article directory submissions is that you can take the same article and author bio and re-use them over and over again.

What you can do is to 'cut-and-paste' the article and post the article to a list of article directories (when in doubt – use Google).

Occasionally, you may find the process too tedious; you can outsource it to someone else for a low price of $27-37 dollars to submit that article for you to a few hundred directories.

If your article is well written, employing this outsourcing method will send a HUGE surge of traffic to your website so you must be prepared. This will not last forever because the articles do not remain on the top page all the time.

Make sure that you are not too 'sales pitchy' about your product or your website because some article directories are particular about the quality of the articles. They are after all, looking for quality content, not another sales letter.

- **Let Others Sell Your Topnotch Ebooks**

If you have your very own E-product, you can easily submit your product to a high-traffic membership site that provides quality content.

The concept is also similar to blog and article contributors except that it takes it up a notch to E-book creation.

The nature of these content membership sites requires new content to be added in from time to time.

What better way to get your own product in front of the eyes of thousands of resellers and Internet marketers who can't wait to sell your product for their own profits (assuming that your product has resell rights to it of course).

The Members Are Your Resellers

If your E-product has master resell rights or unrestricted private label rights, you can be sure that your products will be all over the Internet in no time.

Resellers are always looking for products with a complete sales letter to it. If you have drafted out a sales letter that converts well, you can be sure that a lot of resellers will 'cut-and-paste' your sales letter and your E-book and sell it to their mailing list.

The same goes for certain PLR products as well.

The most important thing for you to remember is this – your books must constantly lead the readers to your websites.

Your links must be placed strategically in the E-books and as your E-books are duplicated all over the Internet, you can be sure to drive plenty of new visitors to your website – even if they are not in your circle of influence!

- **Tap into Forum Traffic**

Your Signature

A signature on the forum is something like a P.S. at the bottom of a forum post and it used as an advertisement for any website you are promoting. You can push forum traffic to your network marketing sites as well.

The signature is automatically inserted into some emails but it works very well in high traffic forums as well.

This is one of the best sources for free traffic that you can utilize. Here's how:

Write a one-liner description about yourself and place the URL of your site right beneath it.

E.g. Jimmy Sloth – Internet marketer and free traffic expert.

(Website)

The Right Niche

One of the best ways to search for the right niche is to do a simple search on Google.

Find the niche you are targeting and enter the keyword followed by the word 'forum'.

(For example: if you are looking for visitors to check out your cooking website, do a search for the word cooking forum).

You will see a list of forums that you can tap into. Find the topic that everyone is talking about or asking a lot of questions.

These people are your gold mine! The reason why they keep asking these questions is because answers have yet to surface and this will be your chance to show them what your website has to offer!

Sign up as a forum member and start contributing as a regular. After a while people will start noticing you and they will start replying to your messages. Some of them will click on your link and it will lead them to your website.

Certain forums also allow forum members to post their offers on the forum as well.

CHAPTER 7- BUILDING THE COURAGE NEEDED FOR SUCCESS

Feelings of low confidence can be corrected with the element of courage being fostered. Though commonly assumed the element of confidence in somehow connected to the feeling of inadequacy this is not always true as other domineering factors can also contribute to the lack of confidence.

One way of developing confidence and courage is to mentally and physically force one's self to face the situation or person as best as they are capable of.

By doing so the individual is able to practice exercising these elements and eventually with consistent practice the elements of confidence and courage will be better develop and come more easily.

Taking action in any way will help rather than to choose to avoid the situation at hand. The practice of taking action also helps to encourage the individual to mentally and physically prepare for any possible changes that could occur to hamper the individual's efforts.

Distancing oneself from people who would rather put them down than encourage is also something that should be seriously considered when trying to build these two elements within oneself.

Finding opportunities to exercise these qualities will allow the individual to learn to adopt being confident and courageous instinctively.

Understanding and accepting that it may not always be easy to exercise either of these elements is also one way showing courage.

Courage is not always about action; it may sometimes be better if the strength and will did not to react to something.

Why Do You Need It?

Confidence is a highly rated necessity in the network marketing arena. If there is no confidence in the product or the service being promoted is will eventually become clear to the potential customer and the sale will not be made.

Not having the confidence to promote the business will also bring about similar negative results. In order to achieve the vision set at the onset of the business exercise all involved should learn to develop the individual confidence capacity to equip them to be strong in the face of any adversity or challenges.

The companies who understand the importance of the confidence ingredient will encourage their employees to attend as many training sessions and they organize.

These sessions will help to teach or guide the participants on how to develop their own individual confidence levels. Learning to focus on the future and the goals set to be achieved in that future will encourage those involved to look beyond their strengths and tap into the confidence levels that can bring about even more strength to face anything and everything.

Having plans in place that are both realistic and achievable will allow for the development of natural confidence in the individual. Goals that are too demanding or unrealistic may work adversely against the element of nurturing confidence thus the need for network marketers to identify the differences. Sometimes confidence is built through the actual exercising of something personally.

Observing how more experienced marketers handle situations will also help the individual confidently deal with matters by duplicating what was observed.

• Believe in Your Product and Company

A potential prospect will be able to read into the body language and presentation of the individual who does not completely believe in the product's or company's merits.

Trying to promote something to someone with the element of belief missing in that promotion exercise will not bring forth the desired positive effects of revenue earned.

Most potential customers will closely observe the presenter and if there is even a hint of lack of belief in the product being promoted the probability of the sale becoming a success will be quite slim.

Learning to project the sense of belief in what is being promoted will help create the circumstances and compelling feeling of the customer to seriously consider making a committed purchase.

The key is to develop this belief system to its optimum level so that it becomes an obvious part of the person and presentation.

Sometimes writing down the points that are causing the disbelief will allow those involved to have a better picture and then address the disbelief element separately and intellectually and try to change the perception until some level of belief is achieved.

Likewise adopting the same method to visualize the benefits and qualities that contribute to the belief in the product or business will help to further reinforce the positive confidence in the said product or business.

Although this may seem a rather trivial or silly exercise, it has been known to further strengthen the individual's stand on certain points.

You will be able to confidently face your customers because you firmly believe on your product and your company's capabilities in a demeanor that cannot be matched for its merits.

• Communicate Effectively

Effective communication can make a big difference in the quality of the approach content and style of an individual which in turn will either make or break the endeavor one has ventured into.

Effective communicators usually eventually develop higher levels of confidence on which most successful businesses are built.

Taking the time to fine tune the basics of communication material will be a good start. Communicating well grammatically is always preferred as this will be well received and impress the listener as compared to someone who is ill equipped grammatically.

Along with this the information that is being communicated should be done as plainly and clearly as possible. Communicating in terms and using jargon that the listener may not understand will eventually cause the listener to lose interest in what is being said, thus making the whole exercise an absolute waste of time.

Being good communicators also means being able to listen well. It does not only focus on the ability to speak well. Failing to be a good listener will lead to the responding communication material being off the point being addressed and so not really addressing the issues being queried or discussed.

CHAPTER 8- OUT-THINK COMPETITION

Often today the term think outside the box is mentioned at various times and in various contexts. The old tried and true methods largely depended on everyone following a set pattern or train of thought to achieve anything.

Exploring and taking risks were almost unheard of and certainly discouraged. Today most companies willingly encourage or even challenge all their employees to think outside the box. The results of which have proven to be phenomenal.

Here are some tips of how to think outside the box:

• Thinking for one's self is often not tapped into enough. People tend to fear the unknown thus preferring to follow the norm, but thinking outside the box requires the individual to explore and venture beyond the norm. There is some level of invigoration felt when this freedom is allowed and encouraged.

- Learning to question anything and everything is also another way of exploring things outside the box. Making it necessary to accept everything heard, read or told is no longer the expected medium of behavior. Questioning means to exercise one's own perception of things which can be surprisingly different from the masses. This difference can in turn bring about new and more innovative and beneficial elements that would greatly change the direction of any endeavor for the better.

- Making a conscious effort to look beyond what is visible and envision what could be is another way of cultivating the out of the box thinking process. Being quick to decide on what is obvious may in fact cause the individual to lose the sense of adventure which looking beyond may unfold.

- Though seemingly basic, the idea of recording thoughts and ideas if often overlooked. Making this a habit would not only help the individual remember fleeting ideas but could also create the birth of ideas that would be both brilliant and useable.

Experiment Every Once in a While

Having an open mind approach when it comes to facing anything is a good and beneficial personality trait to develop. There is always danger in not wanting to be open to new ideas or expansions that may create tumulus changes in life. Without change there is no room to grow and improve thus causing the individual to be left behind in the face pace world of today.

In the business arena there is always the need to explore new ideas and ways to make any venture a phenomenal success and by trying out new ideas, things, applications and other innovative elements, the percentage of making the venture more successful and relevant makes it worth the risk.

It can sometimes be quite a challenge to make these changes and adopt new and unfamiliar ideas and ways of approaching elements that would otherwise have been viewed as routine but there is a necessity to consciously venture into making the effort to try.

Developing a mindset that is willing to address this fear would help to allow the individual to first try out making smaller and perhaps less significant changes.

As the confidence level builds the changes attempted can take on a more significant form thus creating a slower but still more adventurous outlook.

There may be a need to actually focus on growth in a certain area before the individual is willing to try new things.

Focusing on the need to ensure growth in that particular area will encourage the individual to seek alternatives, methods currently adopted by others, newer untried methods and anything that would be considered different.

Practice, Practice, Practice

Nothing beats practice when it comes to wanting to excel in a certain area. This fact has been an accepted and undisputed ideal since way back when. Taking this particular nugget of truth and applying it to the various platforms within the individual's life is not only wise but also worth considering for the merits it promises.

Most people function on automatic for most of their daily life cycles and this can only be done with some level of practiced measures that have been fined tuned over time.

The ability to further enhance any given practice requires the practiced effort of the conscious mind and body working together.

However there are some quarters that are of the opinion that doing things over and over again constitutes some level of laziness seeping into the equation.

This is as yet a hotly disputed and debated fact. Still the concept of practice makes perfect is very much encouraged and a sought after mode of thought.

When it comes to delivering a business idea to a potential prospect, continued practice will yield the desired positive results of being confident and fluent in the delivery of the information.

This ideal can only be reached with the famous practice makes perfect attitude and application. Delivering sales pitches and other material that requires the presenter to be able to handle any interruptions without losing their train of thought is also done because of the practice made perfect exercise.

Most people find some comfort in rehearsing the presentation as frequently as possible as they perceive this to help them better improve on their general delivery, content and style.

There are several different definitions and types of practice methods but all point to the same end of being able to be better prepared for any probabilities and giving optimally presented matter.

Generally people singularly focus on the practice makes perfect style to ensure mistakes are kept to a minimum or none at all.

ABOUT THE AUTHOR

Leanne Toinette Higgins was born on March 10, 1976 to a rich American family. She was the daughter of a successful business owner in Idaho. Leanne had everything that she wanted when she was growing up – everything delivered on a silver platter.

Her parents divorced when she was 13 years old so she moved to Washington with her mother but visited her dad frequently, particularly on summers.

In college, Leanne took up business marketing with the intention of establishing her own business like her father. Unfortunately, she wasn't able to finish the degree because of her high-risk pregnancy. Now a mother and a wife, Leanne still continues her dream of earning more than enough for her family through network marketing.

www.ingramcontent.com/pod-product-compliance
Lightning Source LLC
Chambersburg PA
CBHW070904070326
40690CB00009B/1984